Grant Hill: The Inspiring Story of One of Basketball's Most Resilient Forwards

An Unauthorized Biography

By: Clayton Geoffreys

Table of Contents

Foreword

When Grant Hill retired in 2013, it marked the end of a long NBA career. While many remember Hill as an injury prone forward who struggled to even play a full season as a member of the Orlando Magic, Grant Hill was once a first-option. Grant was the man when he played for Detroit. Although his ankle injuries plagued him for much of the early 2000s, Grant Hill ultimately persevered through the countless surgeries, evolving into a seasoned veteran who consistently contributed to his squads. As a member of the Suns and Clippers, Hill revitalized his career. He may have never returned to the original form he once had as a Detroit Piston, but his road to recovery in order to become the player he became in the latter half of his career is truly an inspiring one that teaches you that no matter what the odds are, and no matter what people are telling you to do, sometimes you just need to keep your head and keep trying until something starts going your way. Thank you for downloading *Grant Hill: The Inspiring*

Story of One of Basketball's Most Resilient Forwards. In this unauthorized biography, we will learn Grant Hill's incredible life story and impact on the game of basketball. Hope you enjoy and if you do, please do not forget to leave a review!

Also, check out my website at claytongeoffreys.com to join my exclusive list where I let you know about my latest books and give you goodies!

Cheers,

Clayton Geoffreys

Visit me at www.claytongeoffreys.com

Introduction

There are few sports leagues today as grueling as the NBA.

The NFL may be tougher per individual game, but they play just 16 games, with a normal rest of 1 week between games. Soccer's Premier League may test its athletes to the limits with its lack of commercial breaks and constant activity, but even they just play 38 games in a season which lasts from August to April. The NBA plays 82 games, with teams sometimes playing back-to-back games and few days of rest over the course of a season. Then there are two additional months of playoffs, where a championship team will play somewhere between 16 and 28 additional games.

Given the physicality of the NBA as well as the strain of the long season, the most important quality an athlete can possess is the ability to stay healthy. It does not matter how high you can jump, or how well you can shoot or pass, if your body is unable to handle the strain of the NBA. That simple fact has left a dark and saddening stain on the career of Grant Hill, a potential all-time great whose brilliant career was derailed by an ankle that would not heal.

The particularly tragic part of Hill's injury is that it could have been avoided. If he had listened to the screams of pain from his body which warned him that it could not take much more, he could have avoided the ankle injury which destroyed his career of greatness. But Hill chose to keep playing – partly out of pride, but partly out of a desire to avoid being hated.

In a sense, Hill's high moral character ended up destroying his career. But at the same time, that same character enabled him to persevere where others would have lost themselves to despair. Hill worked and worked to prove that he still belonged in the league, and managed to carve out a respectable niche for himself even after his many surgeries. It was yet another sign of how great he could have been if his body had been a little kinder to him.

Chapter 1: Childhood and Early Life

Grant Henry Hill was born on October 5, 1972, in Dallas to Calvin and Janet Hill. While many other NBA athletes grow up in broken homes and turn to basketball as a way to escape poverty, Hill was born in a good family. Calvin Hill was a star NFL running back who played for 12 seasons for the Dallas Cowboys, Washington Redskins, and the Cleveland Browns. He won the Rookie of the Year in 1969 and was nominated to the Pro Bowl 4 times. Janet had graduated from Wellesley College, worked as a teacher, and later served her country at the Pentagon when the family moved to Washington DC. The Hill parents did not hesitate to provide their only child with toys and whatever else he needed.

But unlike many rich families who end up spoiling their only child, the Hills took care to instill discipline and good character into Grant. Grant and his friends called his mother "The General" for her tough attitude. Janet Hill made sure that Hill's grades were high and that he did not waste his time watching television or playing video games. One time, Grant Hill came home too late from hanging out with his friends. Janet asked for his watch and promptly broke it! She stated that since Grant was not using the watch, he did not need it.

While Janet was the disciplinarian mother, Calvin was the fun-loving father. He invited fellow NFL athletes to his house, took the young Grant inside the NFL locker rooms, and played football with his son and friends in the backyard. But while Calvin showed Grant around the NFL, he explicitly forbade his son from playing organized football. Calvin did not want Grant to be constantly compared to his own father and hoped that his son would find his own field, whether in sports, academics, or something else.

But no doubt thanks to his father's genes, Grant grew up as an athletic young man who always had a ball in his hands. He dabbled in soccer, but eventually turned towards basketball. Grant was taller than his peers as a young boy. Because smaller players inevitably hogged the ball and had Grant stand by the rim, he decided to work on the ball-handling and passing skills which become his NBA trademarks – all so he could handle the ball on the local playground! He also followed his father's example and began studying tapes of NBA and college basketball plays all on his own. When father and son went to Georgetown University to watch their basketball games, Grant explained how plays were developing to his father.

Chapter 2: High School Years

By the time Grant Hill entered South Lakes High School in 1986, he had already compiled an impressive basketball resume for his age. He had won in multiple youth tournaments, including one game against youth basketball and future NBA stars Jalen Rose and Chris Webber. He had even beaten some of the older players on the South Lakes High School team.

South Lakes Coach Wendell Byrd took a look at the freshman Hill and decided to instantly place him on the varsity team. But while most athletes would have been excited by the chance, Hill demurred. Hill was more comfortable being one of the crowd as opposed to a vocal leader. He greatly treasured his friends, and worried that they might become jealous should he jump ahead of them. But when his friends told him not worry, Hill joined the varsity team.

Hill did not start off as a star. The South Lakes team lacked height, and Hill was one of the bigger players at

6'3''. He focused on rebounding and hitting shots close to the basket. But as his freshman season progressed, Hill handled the ball and took a bigger role on the team. He averaged just 11 points per game as a freshman, but even then Hill was receiving recruitment letters from colleges. Hill asked Coach Byrd if he could keep the letters in Byrd's office and pick them later in secret. In another example of how he considered the feelings of his peers, he worried about jealous feelings from seeing the freshman already receive college scholarships.

By Hill's sophomore season, he became South Lakes's leader both on and off the court. He averaged 25 points over his sophomore season. Hill developed an all-around game which was nearly impossible to stop. He could shoot, dribble, pass, and had excellent athleticism. He continued his habit of watching tapes of NBA, college, and his own basketball to review how he could improve. Hill continued his excellent play as a junior, and by his senior year was averaging

30 points per game. He led South Lakes to win the district championship for the third straight year, and also won the regional championship. At the end of the season, Hill was nominated as a Parade's All-American. Even though he was 6'8'' by his senior year, Hill spent much of the season playing at the point guard position, sparking instant comparison to NBA great Magic Johnson.

Thanks to Hill's successful high school basketball career, he could pick from any university in the United States. Hill's mother wanted him to go to Georgetown and his father wanted him to go the University of North Carolina. Hill openly refused on the former. In a recruitment visit to Georgetown in his junior year, Georgetown's academic advisor insulted Hill's intelligence by making him read a book out loud and then having him explain its contents. He considered joining North Carolina, but instead chose a different path. In 1990, Grant Hill committed to joining the Duke University basketball team. He graduated from

South Lakes as its most successful athlete ever, and would be nominated to the Virginia High School Hall of Fame in 2003.

Chapter 3: College Years at Duke

Once upon a time, the Duke Blue Devils were not the most hated men's college basketball team in America. Coach Mike Krzyzewski had been coaching at Duke since 1980, but in his first three seasons, the Blue Devils failed to even qualify for the NCAA tournament. Duke achieved some success in the late 1980s behind guard Johnny Dawkins and later power forward and future NBA All-Star Christian Laettner. But after getting drubbed 103-73 in the 1990 NCAA Championship Game by the University of Nevada-Las Vegas (UNLV), Duke was looking for an additional boost.

Grant Hill would provide that boost. The young freshman was instantly inserted into Duke's starting lineup and became an integral cog of the team. He continued to work to be an all-around player, and particularly sought to improve his passing game for the college basketball scene. In Hill's freshman season, he averaged 11 points on 51% shooting as well as 6 rebounds. He was nominated a Freshman All-American for his overall play.

For now, Hill was just a solid piece on the Duke Basketball team. However, he developed a reputation for coming up big in important games. Throughout the 1991 NCAA tournament, Hill was solid in every game but the regional semifinal against Connecticut. In the National Semifinal, Duke faced off against UNLV once again. UNLV was the favorite, but Duke managed to prevail 79-77. Hill was a huge part of that win, as he held swingman Stacey Augmon to 6 points while scoring 11 himself. In the final against Kansas, Hill had one of the most famous dunks in NCAA history, swooping up for the one-handed alley-oop from a pass by point guard Bobby Hurley. Duke prevailed 72-65. It was the school's first NCAA championship.

In Hill's sophomore season, he became a more prominent player for the Blue Devils. His work on his passing game over his freshman year bore results, as he now averaged 4.1 assists along with an improved 14 points and 5.7 rebounds. In the 1992 ACC title game, Hill scored 20 points while going a perfect 8-8 from the field.

The 1992 NCAA tournament would have arguably the finest moment of Hill's entire basketball career. Duke was the favorite to repeat at the beginning of the tournament, and they breezed through their first three rounds. But in the East Regional Finals against Kentucky, the Blue Devils found themselves in the fight of their lives. The game was a close, hard-fought battle throughout and went into overtime. With two seconds left in the overtime period, Kentucky guard Sean Woods drove into the paint and hit a difficult layup to put his team up 103-102. With Duke having to inbound the ball from the opposite end of where they needed to score, their chances of victory looked grim.

During the timeout, Coach Krzyzewski asked Hill whether he could throw the ball 75 feet. In one of the most famous plays in college basketball history, Hill accomplished just that. Channeling the genes of Calvin Hill, Grant threw a pass more suited for a quarterback than a basketball player. The ball landed right into the hands of Christian Laettner, who dribbled once, took the fadeaway shot, and hit the game-winner. Hill finished the game with 11 points, 10 rebounds, and 7 assists, with no assist being more crucial than his final full-court pass. Duke would go on to the NCAA Final, where Hill would prevail over Chris Webber and Jalen Rose yet again. In Duke's 71-51 defeat over Michigan, Hill had 18 points and 10 rebounds.

Duke had won its second straight NCAA championship, the first school to accomplish that since UCLA in 1972 and 1973. However, its chances of a third straight title seemed grim. Laettner, who had scored 31 points while going 10-10 from the field in the memorable game against Kentucky, was leaving for the NBA. With him gone, Hill now became the primary scorer for Duke. While Hill had always deferred to Laettner as a freshman and a sophomore, he stepped into the limelight as a junior with little difficulty. He averaged 18 points on 58% shooting and improved his rebounding once again to 6.4 rebounds. However with Laettner gone, Hill's assists total dropped. Duke finished with 24-8 record and lost in the second round of the NCAA tournament. In the second round against California and freshman point guard Jason Kidd, Hill scored 18 points. In addition to his scoring, Hill was also nominated the top defensive player in all of college basketball and a second-team All-American.

The 1993-94 Duke Blue Devils saw the departure of yet another key player in Bobby Hurley. Duke now became Grant Hill and Grant Hill's supporting cast. At the end of games, Coach Krzyzewski would run the "going to Charlotte" offense, where they would give the ball to Hill and expect him to do something. This highly creative offense worked. Hill led Duke to a 28-6 record, and averaged 17.4 points, 6.9 rebounds, and 5 assists. He also shot 39% from the three-point line, a massive improvement over the past three years. After the disappointing tournament result last year, Hill led Duke back to the NCAA Championship Game. On the way there, Hill had huge games throughout the NCAA tournament, including a 25 points and 5 assists performance in the Final Four against Florida. However, he did struggle in the Championship Game against the Arkansas Razorbacks, and Arkansas won 76-72. Even though Hill failed to win his third NCAA championship in four years, he had had a highly college career. That year, he was a unanimous selection to NCAA All-American first team and nominated the ACC Player of the Year. Shortly after Hill graduated from Duke with a major in history and political science, the school retired his #33 jersey

When Hill later declared for the 1994 NBA Draft, there was no doubt that he would be an extremely high draft pick. The Milwaukee Bucks chose power forward Glenn Robinson with the first pick of the draft, and then the Dallas Mavericks selected point guard Jason Kidd. With the third pick, the Detroit Pistons selected Grant Hill. Hill admitted during the post-draft interview that despite everything he had already accomplished, he felt nervous. Nevertheless, he said that he was prepared to lead the Pistons and felt that making it into the NBA was a dream come true.

Chapter 4: Grant's NBA Career

The Rising Star

When Detroit drafted Grant Hill, it seemed to be another stroke of good luck for one of the most prestigious franchises in the NBA. 4 years earlier, the Pistons had won their second straight championship under the "Bad Boys" label and had repeatedly defeated a young Michael Jordan. But now most of the Bad Boys were gone. Isiah Thomas and Bill Laimbeer had retired, and Dennis Rodman had been traded to the San Antonio Spurs. Only 1989 Finals MVP Joe Dumars remained. The Pistons had young players like Lindsay Hunter and Allan Houston, but Hill would have to step up if Detroit was to return to their former glory.

In addition to the expectations which Detroit placed on Hill, the NBA also hoped that Hill could develop into a future superstar. Thanks to his successful years at Duke and great personality, Grant Hill was already one of the most popular athletes in the NBA. Michael Jordan was still in his first retirement, and no one knew if he would ever return. Hill was instantly talked about as the "next Jordan", but he resented the comparisons. While Jordan was a shooting guard who could score from anywhere, Hill was a small forward who had more of an all-around game. What sense did it make to compare two players whose playing styles were so different, he asked?

On November 4, 1994, Grant Hill made his NBA debut against the Los Angeles Lakers. Even though Los Angeles thrashed Detroit 115-98, Hill had 25 points, 10 rebounds, 5 assists, and 3 blocks. In his first six NBA games, he scored above 20 points in all of them. Fans across the NBA fell in love with Hill's athleticism, unselfishness, and good-guy image. In 1995, he was the first NBA rookie to lead the league in All-Star fan votes. At the 1995 All-Star Game, Hill played for 20 minutes and scored 10 points.

Hill continued to improve as the season went on. On March 19, 1995, he scored above 30 points for the first time against the Golden State Warriors. He then went to score 30 points or more 5 more times over the remainder of the regular season. Hill finished the regular season averaging 19.9 points, 6.4 rebounds, and 5 assists that season. He shared the Rookie of the Year along with Jason Kidd.

Despite Hill's impressive performance, the Pistons only won just 28 games due to a lack of size. During the offseason, Detroit drafted center Theo Ratliff to improve their weak frontcourt, signed former All-Star power forward Otis Thorpe, and counted on improvement from their young players. They also brought in Coach Doug Collins, an old-school coach who declared to Hill that he needed to be even more assertive.

In Hill's sophomore year, he continued to improve and lead the Pistons. His scoring stayed around 20 points, but he grabbed almost 10 rebounds per game and also had 7 assists, more than any non-point guard in the league. He was never someone who could score 40 points any given night, but Hill could get a triple double seemingly whenever he wanted. Outside the court, Hill had become so popular that in 1996, he even beat *Michael Jordan* in the All-Star fan voting! He also was nominated to the All-NBA Second Team for the first time.

Hill was not the only Piston to get better that season. Allan Houston became a top scorer, averaging almost 20 points and shooting 42% from three-point range. Lindsay Hunter also developed into a top shooting point guard. Thanks to the development of Detroit's young players as well as the leadership of Grant Hill and Doug Collins, the Pistons won 46 games and returned to the NBA playoffs as the 7th seed. Unfortunately, they found themselves up against the defending Eastern Conference Orlando Magic in the first round. The deep Orlando team, led by Shaquille

O'Neal and Penny Hardaway, shredded the Pistons and swept them in three games. Grant Hill had a good series and scored 19 points on 56% shooting. But he did not have a moment where he completely took over and led the Pistons to a victory. In Game 3, the only close game of the series, it was Allan Houston who led the Pistons down the stretch. Houston finished with 33 points while Hill had 17.

Detroit rewarded Houston's toughness in the 1996 NBA Playoffs by not offering him a contract and watching as he departed for the New York Knicks. With Houston gone, Grant Hill would need to continue his work as the unquestioned leader of the Pistons. The 1996-97 season would turn out to be his best yet. Hill worked on his finishing ability and improved his ability to draw fouls. He also continued to improve passing game, as his assists managed to increase and his turnovers decreased at the same time. Joe Dumars and Lindsay managed to fill in for Houston's departure, and the Detroit Pistons won 54 games, the highest since they won the championship in 1990. Hill once again made the All-Star Game. At the end of the season, he averaged 21.4 points on nearly 50% shooting, 7.7 rebounds, and 6.8 assists. He also qualified for the All-NBA First Team and placed third in MVP voting behind Jordan and Karl Malone.

The Pistons had the 5th seed and faced off against the Atlanta Hawks in the first round of the NBA Playoffs. The Hawks had a familiar face in Christian Laettner, but also had defensive center Dikembe Mutombo and shooting guard Steve Smith. The Pistons would take a 2-1 lead in the best of five series thanks to 24 points and 8 assists by Hill in Game 3. He would also block Laettner late in the game, thus proving that old college friendships did not matter in the world of the NBA Playoffs. But despite the series lead, Detroit was unable to stop Steve Smith in Game 4 and Hill struggled in Game 5. Atlanta managed to come from behind and prevailed 3-2. Nevertheless, the season was a success for the Pistons. They were still a young team and believed that in due course it would be their time to take over the Eastern Conference.

Despite this optimism, the 1997-98 season would be a disaster. The Pistons went from winning 54 games to 37 despite a lack of serious injuries. There are multiple explanations for this sudden setback. Joe Dumars's age began to catch up with him and the departure of Otis Thorpe was a serious blow to Detroit's weak front court. However, a great deal of the blame can be laid at the feet of Doug Collins. Throughout his 11 seasons coaching the NBA, Collins has consistently shown the ability to instantly get great results out of a team with his tough, hard-nosed attitude. But as the seasons go by, Collins's approach inevitably inspires resentment and frustration as his players who get tired of his ceaseless complaining. The result is a locker room meltdown and a disappointing season in his third or fourth year coaching a team, and this is exactly what happened in Detroit. Even the mild-mannered Hill commented that thanks to Collins, "I didn't enjoy going to practice, I didn't enjoy going to games."

Thanks to Detroit's disappointing start, Collins was fired after 45 games and replaced by Alvin Gentry, who had coached just 36 NBA games before taking up this position. The Pistons continued to struggle under him, and the local and national press began to blame Grant Hill. Hill had yet another season where he passed the ball better than any non-guard in the league and routinely grabbed triple doubles. But while sportswriters had once praised Hill for his humble and friendly personality, they now began to wonder whether Grant Hill had the toughness needed to lead the Pistons to a championship or at least the second round of the NBA Playoffs.

Hill was spurred on by the new criticism to prove that they were wrong. He got into the best shape of his career and waited for the 1998-99 NBA season to begin. The season was delayed by a lockout, but with

Michael Jordan now in his second retirement, the field was wide open for the next team to come in and take Chicago's place atop the NBA world. In Hill's third game of the season against the Washington Wizards, he scored a career-high 46 points. The Pistons rebounded from their disappointing 1997-98 season and finished with a 29-21 record. Once again, they finished with the 5th seed in the Eastern and again found themselves facing the Atlanta Hawks. Christian Laettner was no longer a member of the Hawks. In fact, he had been traded to the Pistons, though he was now a shell of his past glory thanks to a torn Achilles tendon. But Atlanta still had Steve Smith and Dikembe Mutombo. The series lasted five games, but the first four games were all blowouts either in favor of Detroit or Atlanta. Hill had some strong performance, such as a 26 points, 8 assists, and 7 rebounds in Game 1. However, he faded down the stretch in the deciding Game 5, and Atlanta prevailed to win the game and the series 87-75.

Grant Hill continued to work on improving his game, and the 1999-2000 was arguably the finest of his career. The biggest improvement which he showed was a new three-point shot. While Hill had possessed an excellent mid-range jumper since he entered the NBA, he had made only 22 three-pointers in his first 5 seasons in the NBA. In the 1999-2000, Hill made 34. While Hill still remained only an average three-point shooter at less than 35 percent, the threat of the three opened up room in the paint for him to drive. Hill had always been a point forward capable of doing anything. Now he became a deadly scorer as well. In a stretch of four games in six nights in January 2000, Hill scored 40 points or more in three of them. In what would become his final season as a NBA superstar, he scored 25.8 points per game along with 6.6 rebounds and 5.2 assists. He once again made the All-Star Team and the All-NBA Second Team for the third straight year.

But despite Hill's improvement, Detroit won only 42 games that season. Jerry Stackhouse had become a dynamite scorer in his own right, Lindsey Hunter remained an excellent three-point shooter, and Christian Laettner began to recover from his torn Achilles. But Joe Dumars had retired, and Detroit had no center who could defend the paint. Even Hill, despite his many talents, was only an average defender. Detroit was one of the best offensive teams in the league, but they were also one of the worst defensive teams. As the season ground on and the Pistons continued to disappoint, Hill began to consider his options for the 2000 offseason. He would be a free agent at the end of the year, and would be free to sign with another team which could provide him with more help to win a championship.

The Injury

But on April 15, 2000, Grant Hill's career would be forever changed. He had begun suffering ankle problems around mid-March, but chose to persevere through the pain. But in a game against the Philadelphia 76ers, Hill sprained his left ankle. He was helped off the floor, and considered resting it. However, Hill was pressured into doing otherwise. One of the greatest moments in Detroit Pistons history was when point guard Isiah Thomas continued to play on a badly sprained ankle in Game 6 of the 1988 NBA Finals against Magic Johnson's Los Angeles Lakers. Despite the injury, Thomas scored 25 points in the fourth quarter and nearly led the Pistons to their first championship. The Detroit fans and media instantly contrasted Thomas's perseverance with Grant Hill's decision to sit out. They accused Hill of resting his body while he prepared to depart Detroit in free agency. Even the Pistons doctors questioned whether Hill was truly injured. Throughout his entire life, Hill had always deferred to others. Now despite the screams of pain from his body, he decided to suit up and play in the 2000 NBA Playoffs against the Miami Heat.

It would be the greatest mistake of his life. In Game 1, Hill had a poor game by his superstar standards as he shot 3-9 from the field. In Game 2, Hill played for much of the first half, but then in the second quarter felt a pop and could no longer play. After the game, Detroit's team doctors confirmed the worst. Grant Hill's ankle was broken. The Pistons played Game 3 without him and were swept by the Heat.

In the 2000 offseason, Hill entered free agency. The New York Knicks and Chicago Bulls immediately contacted him, but the Orlando Magic quickly became the frontrunners to sign him. After losing their championship duo of Shaquille O'Neal and then Penny Hardaway, the Magic were looking to build a new core. They had managed to assemble enough cap space to sign two free agents to the maximum level contract. Orlando hoped to pry Hill from the Pistons and Tim Duncan from the San Antonio Spurs to create a new champion duo. They made serious overtures to both players under the label of "Imagine..." and showed them the best of the city and the Florida nightlife. Duncan chose to stay with the San Antonio Spurs, and

Orlando switched to focus on rising star Tracy McGrady. Hill liked the idea of playing in Florida as well as the idea of playing alongside McGrady. On August 3, 2000, the Detroit signed and traded Hill to the Orlando Magic for a few small role players, including an undrafted defensive player named Ben Wallace. Hill would earn $93 million over the next 7 years.

But while the Magic were willing to spend nearly $100 million on Hill, they were seemingly uninterested in making absolutely sure that Hill's ankles had fully recovered. Hill's doctor had declared that he should not participate in basketball-related activities until December. For some reason, neither Orlando nor Hill ever got this message. Hill was playing pick-up games by Labor Day, participated in training camp and preseason games, and started Orlando's first game of the season. He had 9 points and 10 assists. When the doctor found out in the next day's newspaper, he was furious. But the damage had already been done. Hill played just an additional three more games that season before his ankle kept him off the floor once again. In January 2001, he underwent additional ankle surgery which ruled him out for the rest of the season.

Hill continued to work on his rehab, and by some accounts worked too hard and thus threatened his ankle's health. However, by 2003, a familiar pattern had developed. Hill would be ready by the start of the 2001-02 and the 2002-03 season. He would play for a few games and at times look like the old Hill who had been a franchise leader for the Detroit Pistons. But he was never capable of playing like his normal self for long stretches, and by January his left ankle would act up again. He would undergo an ankle surgery and his season would be over. Hill lasted just 14 games in 2001-02 and 29 games in 2002-03.

The 2003 ankle surgery promised to be Grant's last. Doctors had come to the conclusion that Hill's ankle was healing incorrectly. They proposed re-breaking and realigning it to his leg to prevent that from happening again. The surgery was deemed a success, but one week later, Hill suffered from a fever and convulsions. His wife rushed him to the hospital, where they discovered that Hill had contracted a severe bacterial infection during the surgery called MRSA. Hill was fortunate in that the infection had not spread to the bone or his blood; had it done so, the infection could have become life-threatening. As it was, Hill was hospitalized for a week and had to be hooked up to an IV machine three times a day for about six months. He was instantly ruled out for the entire 2003-04 season.

But even though the infection was horrible, in a sense it proved to be a blessing in disguise. One reason why Hill's ankle had failed to properly recover for the past three seasons was that Hill kept trying to rush back onto the court. Thanks to the infection, his ankle now had had all of the time needed to properly recover. But while Hill was feeling better than ever before at the beginning of the 2004-05 season, the Magic had dramatically changed since Hill had signed that contract four years earlier. Tracy McGrady had developed into a true superstar in Hill's absence and had made the All-NBA First Team in 2002 and 2003. However, McGrady was no longer interested in waiting for Hill and requested a trade. In 2004, he was sent to the Houston Rockets in exchange for guards Steve Francis and Cuttino Mobley in addition to forward Kelvin Cato. The duo of Hill and McGrady, which was supposed to lead Orlando back to playoff relevance, had played just 43 games together over four seasons.

The Magic were now in a transitional period as they figured out what to do next. In addition to Francis, who had made the All-Star Team in 2004, the Magic also had 2004 #1 draft pick Dwight Howard. As Howard had been drafted out of high school, it would take him some time to become the dominant center that we know him today. Amidst this period of confusion, Hill stepped in to be a leader. The ankle no longer bothered him at all. While Hill was now 32 years old and had lost much of his athleticism, he still remained a highly effective player. Hill's enduring popularity as well as his inspiring comeback from so many injuries and surgeries meant that he was voted to the 2005 All-Star Game. The Magic stayed above a .500 record for most of the season and appeared to be ready to return to the NBA Playoffs behind Hill. But in February, the Magic traded Steve Francis's long-time partner Mobley to the Sacramento Kings. Francis was furious, sulked without Mobley, and the Magic won just 5 of their final 24 games to miss the playoffs.

Hill hoped to regain more of his former glory in 2005-06, but injuries struck again. While it was not his left ankle this time, it was related. Many NBA athletes upon suffering severe injuries will either consciously or subconsciously alter their stance out of fear of reinjuring the affected body part. This change frequently ends up injuring other body parts. In Hill's case, he placed less pressure on his left ankle, which ended up causing a groin strain and later a tear. Hill underwent surgery and rehab to handle the injury, and played just 21 games that. Sports analysts and fans declared that after missing so many games over the years, the 33-year old Hill should just retire. Even Hill seriously contemplated the possibility. He finally decided that if he underwent another major sports surgery, he would retire.

Fortunately for Hill, his 2006-07 season, while not injury-free, would be surgery-free. He played 65 games that season and averaged 14.4 points, 3.6 rebounds, and 2.1 assists in about 31 minutes of play. Dwight Howard had begun to develop into a franchise player and made the All-Star team for the first time that season. But even when healthy, it was clear that Hill was no longer even the second best player on the Magic. Forward Hedo Turkoglu fulfilled the role of point forward which Hill used to play, and Hill's inability to shoot the 3 made him a poor spacing option alongside Dwight. The Magic finished with a 40-42 record and grabbed the eighth seed in the Eastern Conference. In Hill's first playoffs since his days as a Piston, he found himself facing the Pistons. Hill played better during than the playoffs and nearly led the Magic in scoring with 15 points per game. But the Pistons easily swept Orlando in four games. At the end of the season, Grant Hill's mammoth 7-year contract finally came to an end. He had signed it looking to lead Orlando to a championship. Now at the end, he had to wonder whether any team would accept him at all.

Rejuvenation in Phoenix

On July 11, 2007, Grant Hill chose to sign with the Phoenix Suns for about $2 million. While he was no longer a star at age 35, Hill managed to revitalize his career as a role player with the Suns. Phoenix's warm and dry climate helped, but it was the Suns training staff which monitored Hill and ensured that he could continue to play in the NBA. Thanks to them, Hill managed to play 70 games that year, the highest since he left the Pistons. In 2008-09, Grant Hill at age 36 managed to play all 82 games for the first time in his entire career. In a way, Hill's years of injuries helped him during his time with the Suns. Since he had spent so much time sitting on the bench, his body lacked the wear and tear that was typical of a 35-year old NBA player.

Phoenix's attack revolved around point guard Steve Nash, but Hill functioned as a backup ball handler and shot creator when defenses collapsed too heavily on Nash. He also returned to developing his three-point shot. After his decent campaign from long range in his final season with the Pistons, Hill had made just 9 three-pointers in his seven years with the Magic. Phoenix's run and gun offense gave Hill more chances to shoot threes, and he averaged 32% from long range in his first two seasons with the Suns.

While Hill slowly improved, the Suns struggled during his first two years. They were eliminated in the first round of the playoffs in 2007-08 and then failed to make the playoffs in 2008-09 despite winning 46 games. Shaquille O'Neal left during the offseason, and analysts believed that Phoenix's run at a championship was over. However, the Suns managed to revitalize themselves during the 2009-10 season, and Hill was a significant contributor to this turnaround. His three-point shooting jumped to an excellent 44%. He also loved the chemistry on a Suns team which played together, and later described the team as one of the best memories of his career. Phoenix won 54 games that season, and defeated the Portland Trail Blazers in six games in the first round of the playoffs. For the first time in his career, Grant Hill had gotten past the first round. He had been in the starting lineup and averaged 8 points and 8.3 rebounds during the series. The Suns advanced all the way to the Western

Conference Finals, where they lost to the eventual champion Los Angeles Lakers in six games.

That season turned out to be the last hurrah for Steve Nash's Suns. Amare Stoudemire left for the New York Knicks during the offseason, and the Suns management failed to provide Nash a second star to play with. Consequently, Hill took on a bigger role in Phoenix's 2010-11 offense. While the Suns bounced around with additional wings such as an aging Hedo Turkoglu or Vince Carter, Hill provided a steady scoring presence on the team. He continued to remain healthy and played 80 games that season. He also averaged 13.2 points per game that season, the highest during his time as a Sun. But despite Hill's contribution, the Suns dropped from making the Western Conference Finals to winning 40 games and failing to make the playoffs.

At 39 years old, Hill began to contemplate retirement, but he above all wanted to win the championship which had eluded him throughout his career. After a final season with the Phoenix Suns where his health finally began to fail him, Hill signed with the Los Angeles Clippers in 2012. The Clippers, who had reached the second round of the playoffs the previous year, were seeking to improve their wing depth to play alongside star point guard Chris Paul and rising power forward Blake Griffin. However, Hill began to suffer from injuries once again, this time to his right knee. He did not play until January and then played just 29 games during the 2012-13 season. Hill averaged just 3 points on 38% shooting. His only noteworthy accomplishment was when New York Knicks power forward underwent season-ending surgery, Hill became the oldest player in the NBA. It was still impressive for a player who had been seriously contemplating retirement 7 years earlier.

But after the Clippers lost in the first round and the 2012-13 season was over, Hill contemplated retirement once again. He still had one more year worth $2 million with Los Angeles, and could have just sat back for the 2013-14 season and collected his paycheck. But Hill decided otherwise. On June 1, 2013, Hill went on TNT's *Inside the NBA* and declared: "I'm done. I'm officially retired." He had played for 19 seasons and over 1000 games, but it was time for him to move on.

Chapter 5: Hill's Personal Life

There are few athletes who have such a notable yet wholly positive life off the basketball as Grant Hill. Hill was one of the most celebrated and marquee athletes of the 1990s and was the face of billboards and commercials everywhere. But unlike most NBA athletes who are best known for their work with Nike and Adidas, Hill became most famous for his relationship with SpritChae. The soft drink company released several quirky and humorous commercials which poked fun at many of the conventions of advertising. For example, one Sprite commercial asked whether a kid drinking Sprite would be able to defeat Grant Hill in a basketball game. The answer, contrary to what one might expect from a commercial, turned out to be "absolutely not." Hill also participated in commercials for shoe company Fila and starred in one of ESPN's *This is SportsCenter* advertisements, where he showed off his skills with the piano.

Hill also has spent a great deal of time promoting various causes. He grew up in a Democratic household and his mother used to work alongside the Clinton family. He donated thousands of dollars to the Obama and Kerry campaigns. Outside from the political world, Hill also has donated money and time to causes such as ending homophobic slurs in daily life, promoting literacy, and stopping the spread of the MRSA infection which nearly killed him in 2003. In 2014, Hill donated $1.25 million to Duke University to improve not just its athletic facilities, but to the Trinity College of Arts and Sciences as well. He had also donated $1 million to his old school back in 2000 to support scholarships for students on the men's basketball team.

But even though Hill has such a positive image and has done so many good things throughout his life, he has not been able to entirely avoid controversial moments. In 2011, ESPN released a documentary on the famous "Fab Five", the 1990s Michigan men's basketball team which became famous and infamous across the United States. In the film, Michigan player Jalen Rose labeled black players like Hill who went to Duke "Uncle Toms" and other members of the Fab Five openly insulted. Grant Hill responded by writing a column which was published by the *New York Times.* In the column, Hill talked about the importance of education, took issue with the claim that black Duke basketball players like himself and Shane Battier had somehow "sold out their race", and cautioned the Fab Five against "stereotyping me and others they do not know in the same way so many people stereotyped them back then for their appearance and swagger." After some additional comments back and forth between the Fab Five and Hill, the two groups reconciled shortly afterwards.

Over his many years in the NBA, Hill has been one of the best role models for anyone who wishes to look up to a NBA player. He has continued his work as an honorable man, regardless of those who may disagree with him may think.

Chapter 6: Impact on Basketball

Grant Hill may have been compared to Michael Jordan during his early years as a Piston, but it is another all-time great, drafted nine years after Hill, who serves as a better comparison. LeBron James may not have Grant Hill's finesse and Hill may not have had LeBron's overpowering athleticism. However, both players are small forwards who were just as renowned for their all-around game as much as their scoring ability. Both players were amongst the best in the game. And on a darker note, both players were also criticized for a perceived lack of playoff success. Papers like *USA Today* have noted the similarities between the two, and have wondered whether Grant Hill could have reached the level of LeBron James had it not been for his ankle.

While such a question may seemingly have merit, we must take care not to overly romanticize players whose careers were unexpectedly cut short by injury. As great as prime Grant Hill was, he was simply not in the same class as LeBron James. For example, Grant Hill's highest Player Efficiency Rating (PER) in a season is higher than only one of LeBron's non-rookie seasons. Hill was also not a particularly gifted scorer, as he scored more than 22 points once in his entire career. While Hill could get to the rim and finish, he was held back by the fact that he lacked deep range for most of his career. As noted above, Hill made just 22 three-pointers in his first five years with the Pistons. Even during his best shooting years as a role player for the Suns, he never attempted more than 1.4 threes per game. Hill was an excellent player who wowed the league. But even though he was labeled as the "next Jordan", Hill would probably have never reached the level of Jordan and LeBron even had he managed to stay healthy.

But one does not need to be at the level of those two all-time greats in order to win a championship. As Hill battled injuries in Orlando, Tracy McGrady had developed into one of the premier superstars in the league. Would a healthy Hill and McGrady have been able to lead Orlando into a championship? Given the lack of support around the two stars, perhaps a championship might have been too tall of an order. But it would have been certainly possible, and there is no doubt that Orlando would have gotten past the first round of the playoffs had Hill been healthy. Instead, both McGrady and Hill became infamous for their inability to get past the first round until late in their careers.

In addition to Hill's injury problems, he also suffered from a weak supporting cast throughout his career. In his first six years as a Pistons star, he only played with one All-Star, an aging Joe Dumars. In addition, Detroit's frontcourt was absolutely miserable. Hill's teammates at the power forward and center positions consisted of players like Bison Dele, an aging Otis Thorpe, and a Christian Laettner recovering from a torn Achilles tendon. Even though Detroit's management failed to provide their superstar with the supporting cast that he deserves, they insinuated that Hill was not tough for playing through a badly damaged ankle. They compared him to Isiah Thomas, who had the great fortune of playing with other greats like Dennis Rodman and Bill Laimbeer.

Hill's injuries has meant that his career has been overly romanticized, and we should remember that as great as he was, he was never the best player in the league nor at the level of some of the greatest players in league history. But he was still an excellent player and among the best in the league in his prime. He was cursed not just by his ankle, but by a lack of great teammates until his role player days on the Sun. Perhaps had things been dramatically different, Grant Hill may have been talked about in the same that we talk of Dirk Nowitzki or Carmelo Anthony today. But Hill accepted his misfortune with grace and perseverance, and carved a career for himself years after people proclaimed that he was finished. It is the greatest possible testament to Grant Hill's dedication and character.

Chapter 7: Hill's Legacy and Future

When many all-time greats leave the NBA court for the last time, you cannot help but wonder what they will do now that they have left the game to which they have devoted their lives and bodies. Some athletes never really manage to leave. They hang around the court, attempt an ill-fated comeback, or go play in another foreign league for a time.

Grant Hill does not have that problem. In a way, his years spent sitting the sideline nursing his ankle have helped remind him that there are more important things than basketball. His first child, a daughter named Myla, was born in 2002. Hill observed how Myla helped him take his mind off what were at the time painful basketball memories as well as the state of his ankle. He has stated that while NBA teams have called and asked if he has any interest in returning to the NBA, he has no regrets in leaving when he did. As

Hill described it: "I remember someone telling me, play until the wheels are off. The wheels are off."

That is not to say that Hill has completely abandoned basketball. After retiring from the NBA, Hill works today as a broadcaster for NBA TV. As part of the sports media world, Hill has talked with Tracy McGrady when he attempted his baseball career, helped Kevin Durant cook at Durant's new Oklahoma City restaurant, and showed off his skill with the trombone.

As Hill continues to enjoy his life after the NBA, we should take a look back and admire everything he has accomplished. Perhaps he did not have to struggle to enter the NBA as much as other players who grew up in more difficult circumstances. But once he entered the NBA and cemented his reputation as a star, Hill endured trials which would have made lesser players give up on the sport. Instead, Hill fought and persevered so that his final days would be remembered for his play on the court and not for his time wearing a suit on the sidelines. He spent 19 years in the NBA, something which would have seemed all but impossible when his life was threatened after yet another ankle surgery. Given the level of play needed to make and stay in the NBA, as well as the difficulties he faced that should above all be one of the crowning jewels of his legacy.

Final Word/About the Author

I was born and raised in Norwalk, Connecticut. Growing up, I could often be found spending many nights watching basketball, soccer, and football matches with my father in the family living room. I love sports and everything that sports can embody. I believe that sports are one of most genuine forms of competition, heart, and determination. I write my works to learn more about influential athletes in the hopes that from my writing, you the reader can walk away inspired to put in an equal if not greater amount of hard work and perseverance to pursue your goals. If you enjoyed *Grant Hill: The Inspiring Story of One of Basketball's Most Resilient Forwards* please leave a review! Also, you can read more of my works on *Klay Thompson, Anthony Davis, Stephen Curry, Kevin Durant, Russell Westbrook, Chris Paul, Blake Griffin, Joakim Noah, Scottie Pippen, Kobe Bryant, Carmelo Anthony, Kevin Love, Tracy McGrady, Vince Carter, Patrick Ewing, Karl Malone, Tony Parker, Allen*

Iverson, *Hakeem Olajuwon, Reggie Miller, Michael Carter-Williams, James Harding, John Wall, Tim Duncan,* and *Steve Nash* in the Kindle Store. If you love basketball, check out my website at claytongeoffreys.com to join my exclusive list where I let you know about my latest books and give you lots of goodies.

Like what you read?

If you love books on life, basketball, or productivity, check out my website at claytongeoffreys.com to join my exclusive list where I let you know about my latest books. Aside from being the first to hear about my latest releases, you can also download a free copy of *33 Life Lessons: Success Principles, Career Advice & Habits of Successful People.* See you there!

Printed in Great Britain
by Amazon

14086477R00037